I'M NOT OK
YOU'RE NOT OK

ACTIVITIES FOR
BAD DAYS, SAD DAYS, AND
STARK-RAVING MAD DAYS

COREE SPENCER
+
EMILY NILAND

ABRAMS NOTERIE, NEW YORK

Editor: Samantha Weiner
Designer: Katie Benezra
Production Manager: Rebecca Westall

ISBN: 978-1-4197-4046-6

Text © 2020 Coree Spencer and Emily Niland
Illustrations © 2020 Emily Niland

Cover © 2020 Abrams

Printed and bound in China
10 9 8 7 6 5 4 3 2 1

Abrams Noterie products are available at special discounts when
purchased in quantity for premiums and promotions as well as
fundraising or educational use. Special editions can also be created
to specification. For details, contact specialsales@abramsbooks.com
or the address below.

ABRAMS The Art of Books
195 Broadway, New York, NY 10007
abramsbooks.com

MIX
Paper from
responsible sources
FSC™ C144853

THIS BOOK BELONGS TO:

_____

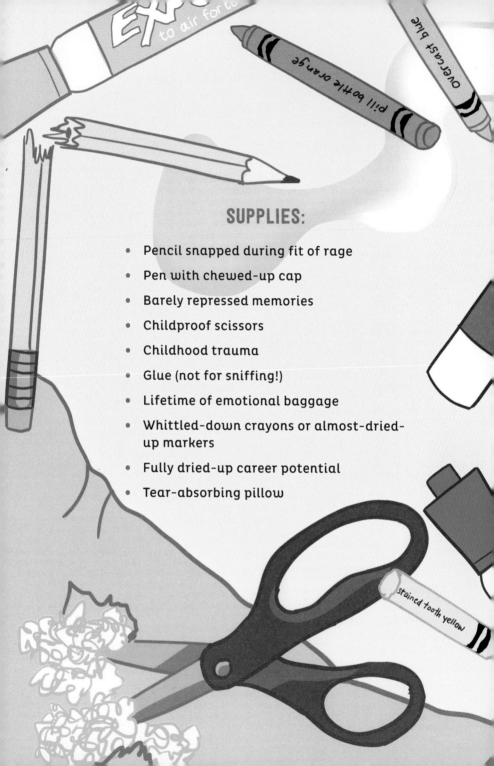

SUPPLIES:

- Pencil snapped during fit of rage
- Pen with chewed-up cap
- Barely repressed memories
- Childproof scissors
- Childhood trauma
- Glue (not for sniffing!)
- Lifetime of emotional baggage
- Whittled-down crayons or almost-dried-up markers
- Fully dried-up career potential
- Tear-absorbing pillow

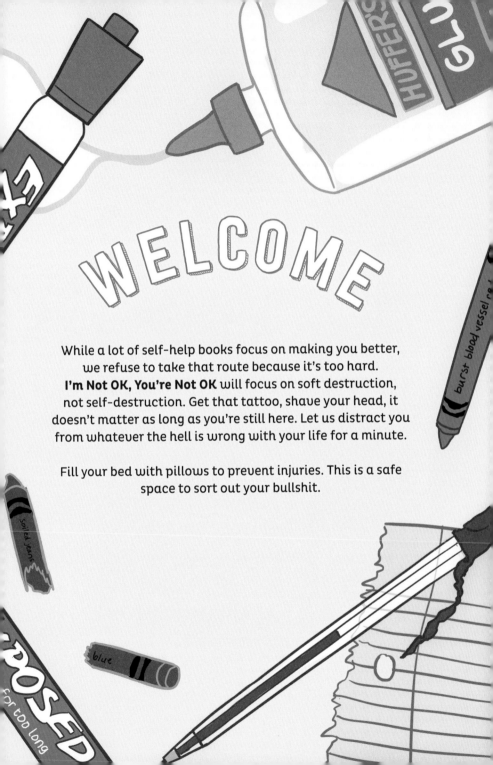

WELCOME

While a lot of self-help books focus on making you better, we refuse to take that route because it's too hard. **I'm Not OK, You're Not OK** will focus on soft destruction, not self-destruction. Get that tattoo, shave your head, it doesn't matter as long as you're still here. Let us distract you from whatever the hell is wrong with your life for a minute.

Fill your bed with pillows to prevent injuries. This is a safe space to sort out your bullshit.

DOWNWARD SPIRAL

It's just a hiccup.   Nobody's perfect.

I'm fine.

I'm doing my best.

Fuck you, I'm doing my best!

You're doing this to hurt me.

STABLE
THOUGHTS &
EMOTIONS

I don't deserve anything good. I am a magnet for abusers.

I'm doing my best, but I still fail. This world is a nightmare.

I'm too
damaged to function.   Ugh, I'm so stupid.

I should just take what I can get.   No one likes me.

I'm too far gone.

WRITE YOUR OWN

Start here

SPIRALIZED THOUGHTS & EMOTIONS

• • • WHAT'S YOUR • • •
ANGER STYLE?

(PLEASE SELECT THE BEST FIT)

☐ **CLASSY**

I'm angry, but I look AMAZING.

☐ **SASSY**

Fuck you, you don't know me, bitch.

☐ **CHRISTMASSY**

I only hate during the holidays.

☐ **RACIST**

It's all because of THEM.

☐ **SEXIST**

It's all because of THEM.

☐ **CLASSIST**

It's all because of THEM.

☐ **LIGHT**

I'm not mad, I'm just disappointed.

☐ **RIGHT**

Obviously, I'm always right.

☐ **FIGHT**

"Seriously, bro, do you want to go?"

YOUR CASTLE

EVERY HOME SHOULD HAVE A NAME!

Use this handy exercise to select the perfect
moniker for your domain.

MONTH YOU WERE BORN

January - The Great

February - Land of the

March - The Big

April - Temple of

May - Palace of

June - Rolling

July - Casa de

August - Mar-a-

September - Chateau

October - Isle of

November - Whispering

December - Manor of

FIRST LETTER OF YOUR LAST NAME

A - Barf

B - Crap

C - Irregular Bowels

D - Cat Litter

E - Isolation

F - Tears

G - Piss Stains

H - Simmering Rage

I - Laziness

J - Ugh

K - Denial

L - Pain

M - Trauma

N - Doom

O - Sadness

P - Toe Fungus

Q - Shame

R - Injustice

S - Garbage

T - Money Trouble

U - Food Poisoning

V - Self-Hatred

W - Nothingness

X - FOMO

Y - Wasted Youth

Z - Open Sores

HOME SWEET HOME

_____   _____
(MONTH)   (INITIAL)

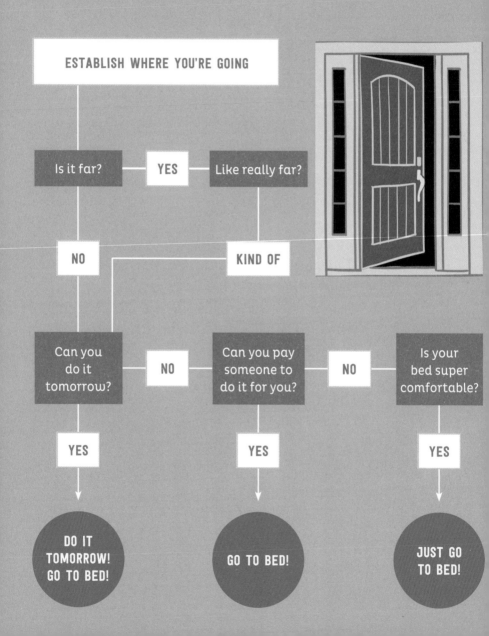

· · · WHAT'S WORTH · · ·
LEAVING THE HOUSE FOR?

(CHECK ALL THAT APPLY)

- ☐ Walking the dog
- ☒ You're hungry
- ☒ Picking up drugs or alcohol
- ☐ Getting cash for drugs or alcohol
- ☐ Super Bowl
- ☐ Comic-Con
- ☐ Holiday party
- ☒ Groceries
- ☐ Mailing rent
- ☒ Stitches removal
- ☐ Military draft
- ☒ Coffee
- ☐ Hair dye
- ☐ Stolen identity
- ☐ New Year's Eve
- ☐ Prescription refill
- ☒ Small fire
- ☒ Large fire

- ☒ Road trip
- ☒ Lobster fest
- ☐ Halloween
- ☒ Bed bugs infestation
- ☐ Camping
- ☒ The cat litter is two weeks old
- ☐ Buying a new game
- ☒ Buying personal hygiene products
- ☐ Power outage
- ☐ No Internet
- ☒ Taking out trash
- ☒ Haircut
- ☒ Psychiatrist appointment
- ☐ Your birthday
- ☒ Your parent's funeral
- ☒ Therapy
- ☐ Deposit check
- ☐ Lightbulbs burned out

A HOUSE MEETING

Follow these guidelines to conduct the ultimate combative house meeting with your roommates and/or loved ones. Remember, this isn't about compromise or resolution—this is about winning.

1.
Be ready with really personal insults that go back years.

2.
Start before everyone has arrived so you can talk about whoever isn't there.

3.
Set a timer for how long each person can speak, but ignore it entirely.

4.
Angriest person talks first. You can determine anger level based on who looks like they could fry an egg from the heat on their forehead.

5.
Anyone who says "I don't want to fight," loses.

6.
If someone mentions your name, immediately begin screaming that they are attacking you.

7.
If you cry, you will be ignored unless you are screaming.

8.
Mirror the person you want to piss off. If they say, "You're hurting me," just say it back. Gaslighting 101!

• • • HOW TO START A FIGHT • • •
ABOUT NOTHING

So you're hungry or bored and are looking to let off some steam. Follow this guide to initiate a real barn-burner of a fight with the nearest human participant. Use these examples to write your own argument starters.

AN ANNOYANCE IN THE ROOM	NONVERBAL ATTACK	VERBAL ATTACK
You can hear them breathing	Bang cabinets to get their attention	"Why does everything have to be so loud?"
You can hear them chewing	Make extremely disgusted face at them	"Were you raised in a barn?"
Temperature is too hot	Let out deep, exaggerated sighs	"Really? You're fine with this?"
Temperature is too cold	Violently wrap yourself in a blanket	"Did you leave the window open again?"
Lights are too bright	Squint profusely	"Do you even care about ambiance?"
Lights are too dim	Use phone flashlight to walk around	"Were you raised in a cave?"

DIY CHORE CHART

Keep track of the day-to-day tasks that will help build a sense of structure in an otherwise chaotic world.

MATERIALS:

- 1 "Do Not Disturb" door hanger
- 1 paintbrush
- 3 paint colors
- Clothespins
- A lifetime of unhealthy coping mechanisms and lowered expectations

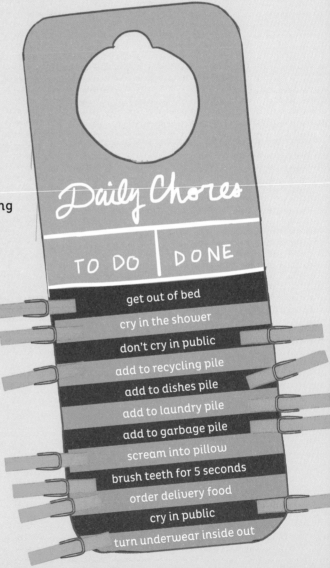

Daily Chores

TO DO	DONE

- get out of bed
- cry in the shower
- don't cry in public
- add to recycling pile
- add to dishes pile
- add to laundry pile
- add to garbage pile
- scream into pillow
- brush teeth for 5 seconds
- order delivery food
- cry in public
- turn underwear inside out

ENNUI MOBILE

Give shape and form to the vague sense of boredom and existential dread by attaching symbols of dull despair to a spinning mobile.

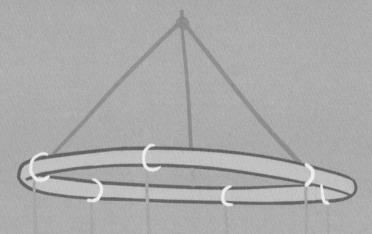

Sock missing its mate

Expired coupon

Empty toothpaste tube

Hair from shower drain

Meeting "notes"

Photo of Ed Sheeran

COLORING BREAK!
FRIDGE OF DOOM

Kind of says it all about your mental state, don't you think?

··· REALISTIC ···
GROCERY SHOPPING

WHAT YOU WANT TO BUY

WHAT YOU ACTUALLY BOUGHT

_____

_____

_____

_____

_____

_____

_____

_____

_____

_____

_____

_____

_____

_____

_____

_____

_____

_____

WOULD YOU RATHER.

Consider each scenario and explain the reasoning behind your choice.

Eat a live snake or cry blood?

_____

_____

_____

_____

Fall into an open sewer or get a tooth pulled with pliers?

_____

_____

_____

Drive a car that's on fire or drink from a toilet?

_____

_____

_____

NAME THAT STAIN

Using your disgusting home as a guide, match the stains to remember what went wrong there! Check the box next to the explanation that is most likely.

RED
- ☐ Wine
- ☐ Lipstick
- ☐ Blood of those who betrayed you

YELLOW
- ☐ Mustard
- ☐ Custard
- ☐ Baby shit

BLUE
- ☐ Blueberries
- ☐ Dish soap
- ☐ Exploded Bic pen

CLEAR
- ☐ Lube
- ☐ Doughnut glaze
- ☐ Tears

ORANGE
- ☐ Nacho cheese
- ☐ Pizza cheese
- ☐ Rust

GREEN
- ☐ Grass
- ☐ Guac
- ☐ Mold

BROWN
- ☐ Chocolate
- ☐ Coffee
- ☐ What was supposed to be a fart

BLACK
- ☐ Squid ink
- ☐ Bong water
- ☐ A portal to another realm

WHITE
- ☐ Mayonnaise
- ☐ Sour cream
- ☐ Whitening toothpaste that dribbled out of your mouth

HOPE FOR THE BEST BUT
ALWAYS EXPECT THE WORST

YOU GET A PROMOTION AT WORK WITH A HUGE RAISE

Best-Case Scenario?   Worst-Case Scenario?

_____   _____

_____   _____

_____   _____

_____   _____

A BELOVED FRIEND COMES TO VISIT FOR A LONG WEEKEND

Best-Case Scenario?   Worst-Case Scenario?

_____   _____

_____   _____

_____   _____

_____   _____

YOU ARE UPGRADED TO FIRST CLASS ON A LONG FLIGHT

Best-Case Scenario?   Worst-Case Scenario?

_____   _____

_____   _____

_____   _____

_____   _____

YOU WIN CONCERT TICKETS TO SEE YOUR FAVORITE BAND

Best-Case Scenario?   Worst-Case Scenario?

_____   _____

_____   _____

_____   _____

_____   _____

FIND THE BIGGEST

DUST BUNNY IN YOUR HOUSE AND GLUE IT HERE

How far have you let things go? Much like the rings of a tree trunk, this helpful benchmark will be a good system for measuring the maturation of your despair.

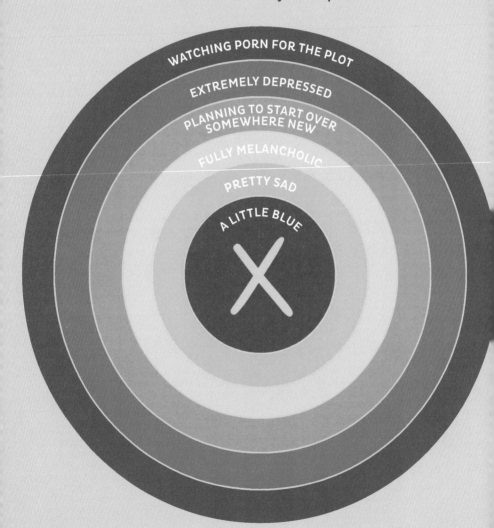

WATCHING PORN FOR THE PLOT

EXTREMELY DEPRESSED

PLANNING TO START OVER SOMEWHERE NEW

FULLY MELANCHOLIC

PRETTY SAD

A LITTLE BLUE

SCAVENGER HUNT

You have 24 hours to complete this (or until whenever you lose motivation)!

☐ Empty water bottle	☐ Fashion mistake	☐ Unfinished to-do list	☐ Anti-itch cream
☐ Loose tooth	☐ Miscellaneous trash	☐ Pimple	☐ Skeleton in the closet
☐ Sticky coin	☐ Dead lighter	☐ Drugs	☐ Crumpled receipt
☐ French fry	☐ Ball of hair	☐ Pants you're too fat for	☐ Dirty underwear

CRYSTALS
••• THAT WON'T HEAL YOU •••

Don't fall victim to the scams perpetrated by the deceptive crystal industry. Learn how to spot these frauds in the wild and guard yourself against their perilous side effects.

HIMALAYAN SALT CRYSTALS
Will cause a spike in blood pressure

TURQUOISE
Suddenly you have a collection of bolo ties

TIGER'S EYE
Always watching and judging

JADE
Will cause you to become even more cynical and apathetic

CRYSTAL METH
Will create more problems

YOUR MOM'S FRIEND CRYSTAL
Will try to drag you to a pilates class

CANDLES

• • • WILL CURE EVERYTHING • • •

Please reference this color-coded guide when buying candles to decorate your home and set your intentions. Harness their healing powers on your journey to personal fulfillment.

FIRE

This candle will burn your house down.

SPIRITUALITY

Ghosts are watching you change clothes.

SUNLIGHT

This will be enough sun for today.

MONEY

You just spent $20 on an organic candle.

FREEDOM

You can just steal candles.

PURITY

This is a boring candle.

DEPRESSION MEALS

When you're too broke for delivery and too fatigued to leave the comfortable isolation of your own home, there are always depression meals! Found in the recesses of your cupboards and refrigerator, these putrid combos will give you the strength to power through another Netflix binge session.

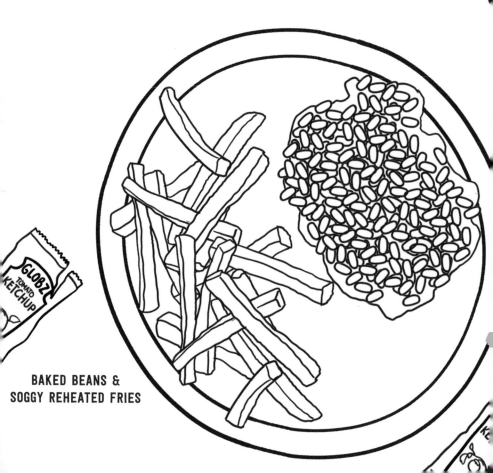

BAKED BEANS &
SOGGY REHEATED FRIES

STALE CHIPS &
GUMMY BEARS

BURNT TOAST
& EXPIRED
PICKLES

WAY

Instead of breaking the dishes, CLEAN the dishes! Write things you hate using condiments and wash them all away!

• • • FILL YOUR OWN • • •
WEIGHTED BLANKET

Scrounge around for whatever items you have on hand
to make a therapeutic weighted blanket. Proven to
alleviate anxiety, this handcrafted body cover will also
help you eliminate any unwanted clutter!

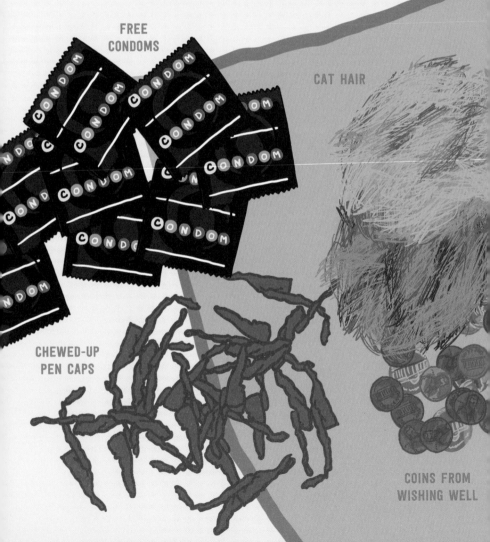

FREE
CONDOMS

CAT HAIR

CHEWED-UP
PEN CAPS

COINS FROM
WISHING WELL

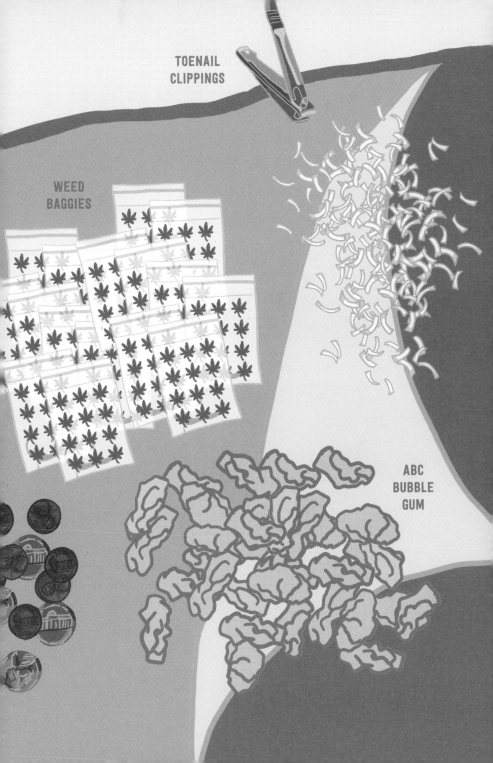

HOPE FOR THE BEST BUT
ALWAYS EXPECT THE WORST

YOU HAVE A CONVERSATION WITH A STRANGER

Best-Case Scenario?

Worst-Case Scenario?

_____   _____

_____   _____

_____   _____

_____   _____

YOU ARE CAST ON A REALITY TELEVISION SHOW

Best-Case Scenario?

Worst-Case Scenario?

_____

_____

_____

_____

_____

_____

_____

_____

YOU DRINK TOO MUCH COFFEE BEFORE BED

Best-Case Scenario?

Worst-Case Scenario?

_____

_____

_____

_____

_____

_____

_____

_____

YOU FIND OUT ONE OF YOUR PARENTS IS A SERIAL KILLER

Best-Case Scenario?

Worst-Case Scenario?

_____

_____

_____

_____

_____

_____

_____

_____

FIND A DOCTOR

RESEARCH DOCTORS

Go online to find therapists or psychiatrists who allegedly accept your insurance and are located even remotely near your home or place of work.

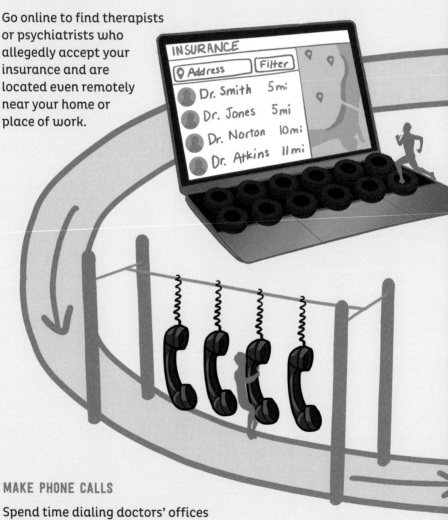

INSURANCE

Address | Filter

Dr. Smith   5mi
Dr. Jones   5mi
Dr. Norton   10mi
Dr. Atkins   11mi

MAKE PHONE CALLS

Spend time dialing doctors' offices to speak to an actual human being. Uh-oh! No one is accepting new patients at this time.

OBSTACLE COURSE

RECEIVE NO CALLS

Constantly check your phone to see if any of the dozens of voicemails you left were returned. They haven't been! Return to start of course.

LEAVE VOICEMAILS

Figure out a good spiel to introduce yourself and inquire about setting up a first-time appointment. Don't forget to leave your phone number!

BETWEEN TWO WAITING ROOMS?

JOGGING ROUTE

• • • OF REGRETS • • •

Wind your way through this maze of bitterness and resentment without running into all the landmarks that comprise the misery of a troubled past.

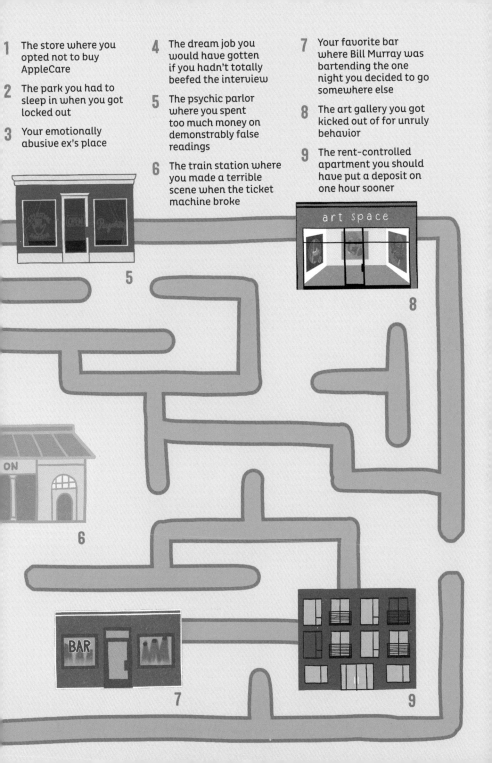

1 The store where you opted not to buy AppleCare

2 The park you had to sleep in when you got locked out

3 Your emotionally abusive ex's place

4 The dream job you would have gotten if you hadn't totally beefed the interview

5 The psychic parlor where you spent too much money on demonstrably false readings

6 The train station where you made a terrible scene when the ticket machine broke

7 Your favorite bar where Bill Murray was bartending the one night you decided to go somewhere else

8 The art gallery you got kicked out of for unruly behavior

9 The rent-controlled apartment you should have put a deposit on one hour sooner

• • • YOUR DEPRESSION • • •
OLYMPIC RECORDS

Mark your progress and go for gold!

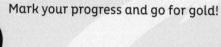

Stayed in same clothes
for _____ days

Stayed in bed
for _____ days

Did not change toilet paper
roll for _____ days

_____ levels won
on toilet

Ordered takeout
_____ meals in a row

_____ seasons streamed
in less than three days

NINJA WORRIER

Respond to the prompts in the boxes below to articulate what personal weaknesses are standing in the way of your happiness and inner peace.

Am I good enough for my career?

Are my thoughts rational?

Will I ever be OK?

Do people still like me?

CARRY THE SYMBOLIC
WEIGHT OF YOUR DEBTS

Build upper-body strength by using the crippling weight of your financial burdens! Write your debts on different-size stones to carry with you wherever you go. These may include student loans, credit cards, mortgage (ha!), or money "borrowed" from family and friends. Debts of gratitude void where acts of kindness are prohibited.

STURDY BACKPACK OF SHAME

Must be carried with
you at all times

**BIG DEBTS
($50,000+)**

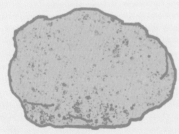

**MEDIUM DEBTS
($1,000–$49,999)**

**SMALL DEBTS
($1–$999)**

STRESS FACTORS

• • • LIKELIHOOD SCALE • • •

Are you making a mountain out of a molehill?
Take some time to assess the likelihood of your worries
actually coming true. Look to the examples on the
chart below and add your own!

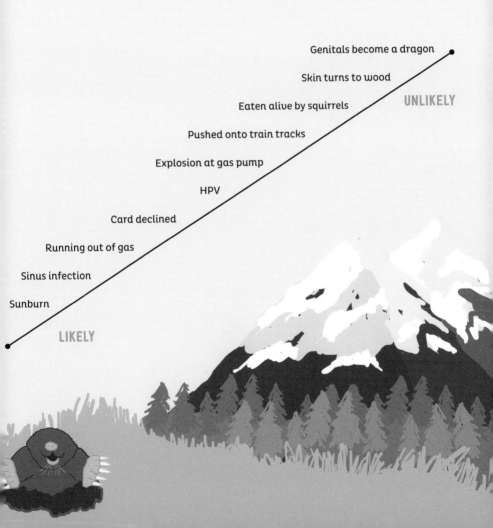

Genitals become a dragon

Skin turns to wood

Eaten alive by squirrels

UNLIKELY

Pushed onto train tracks

Explosion at gas pump

HPV

Card declined

Running out of gas

Sinus infection

Sunburn

LIKELY

COLORING BREAK!
PARTICIPATION TROPHIES

Because you deserve the most for doing the very least,
color in the trophies that you have earned.

MADE IT THIS FAR

PROBABLY NOT
AN ADDICT

DIDN'T CANCEL
PLANS THIS WEEK

DIDN'T CRY TODAY—
WAIT, NEVER MIND

STILL HAVE ONE
FRIEND LEFT

ONLY ORDERED
DELIVERY ONCE TODAY

··· MENTAL HEALTH ···
MERIT BADGES

Cut these badges out, then pin them on your clothes or take them down to the local tattoo parlor to get them emblazoned on your flesh!

Coughs With
Mouth Uncovered

Cancels On
Every Event

Chain-smoker

Blames Bad Luck

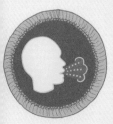

Agoraphobic

Won't Talk
About Sad Stuff

Pees In Containers

Still Their
Inner Child

Unloads On
Strangers

Personality
Is Glasses

Doomsday Prepper

Too Many Pets
To Name

PARENTAL

• • • REPORT CARD • • •

How bad did these people mess you up?

SUBJECT	GRADE
FINANCIAL SUPPORT	
EMOTIONAL SUPPORT	
HEALTH & PHYSICAL EDUCATION	
COMMUNICATION	
HISTORY REVISION	
ATTENDANCE OF IMPORTANT EVENTS	
CONDUCT	
COURTESY	

EXPLANATION OF MARKS

A - Excellent B - Good C - Satisfactory

D - Poor F - Failure

EX-LOVER

• • • REPORT CARD • • •

For when you're thinking of giving them another shot.

SUBJECT	GRADE
FIDELITY	
EMOTIONAL SUPPORT	
CHEMISTRY	
COMMUNICATION	
HISTORY REVISION	
ATTENDANCE TO SEXUAL NEEDS	
CONDUCT	
COURTESY	

EXPLANATION OF MARKS

A - Excellent B - Good C - Satisfactory

D - Poor F - Failure

FEARS

• • • THROUGH THE YEARS • • •

BABY'S FIRST FEARS

_____
_____
_____
_____

**THINGS I'M NOT
AFRAID OF ANYMORE**

_____
_____
_____
_____

MOST IRRATIONAL FEARS

_____
_____
_____
_____

MOST RATIONAL FEARS

_____
_____
_____
_____

**FEARS THAT HAVE
ACTUALLY COME TRUE**

_____
_____
_____
_____

CURRENT FEARS

_____
_____
_____
_____

• • • WEAVE YOUR OWN • • •

WEB OF LIES

Lies You Tell Your Parents

Lies You Tell Your Boss

Lies You Tell Your Partner

Lies You Tell Your Doctor

Lies You Tell Yourself

Lies You Tell Online

Lies You Tell Your Friends

Lies You Tell Strangers

PRESSURE POINTS

Use these never-fail pressure points so you don't scream at anyone today.

FOR ANXIETY

Touch right under your collarbone when your boss calls you into their office.

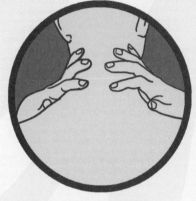

FOR EXHAUSTION

Touch the back of your neck to make your face not look so tired.

FOR CLEARING YOUR HEAD

Touch halfway down the outside of your upper arm to stop looping on how dumb everyone is.

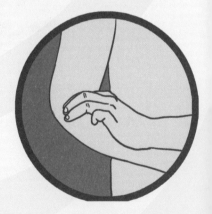

FOR TENSION

Touch the outer edge of the crease of your elbow when your coworker tells racist jokes.

THINGS YOU CAN SQUEEZE FOR
STRESS RELIEF

Easy-to-find relief is literally in your hands.

GRAINS OF RICE

WATER BALLOON

STEERING WHEEL

EMPTY TOILET PAPER ROLL

AIR HORN

REMOTE CONTROL

ROTTEN TOMATO

FINAL NOTICE

666 DROWNING DEBT ST.
CRIPPLING BURDEN, NY
U.S.A.

BILLS

COLORING BREAK!

FRAGILE OBJECTS

THAT CAN BE SMASHED IN A VACANT PARKING LOT

PORCELAIN
FIGURINE

PRICELESS VASE

PIGGY BANK

CHAMPAGNE FLUTE

ICE SCULPTURE

HANDHELD
MIRROR

• • • WEAPONS OF • • •
SOFT DESTRUCTION

Acts of self-sabotage are perfect for being your
own worst enemy! These examples certainly aren't the nuclear option
but can scratch that itch to fuck yourself over. Add your own!

Ask to speak to the manager _____

Procrastinate more often _____

Make promises you can't keep _____

Get too high before family functions _____

Cut off all your hair _____

Eat the entire cake _____

Throw away keepsakes _____

Confess feelings to your crush _____

Tell off a stranger _____

Sleep all day _____

Wear socks with sandals _____

Turn on your read receipts _____

Live Laugh Love

CHAOS ADDICTION

In the unlikely event you find yourself in a calm period of your life, it may be tempting to create your own chaos to feel normal. Here are some suggestions for coping with your newfound serenity instead. Add your own!

Worry about impending doom _____

Wonder if karma is real after all _____

Find a wholesome vice _____

Watch more reality TV _____

Buy a zen garden and destroy it _____

Plan an elaborate bank heist _____

Become a firefighter _____

Focus on your inner demons _____

Freak out over nothing _____

Make disturbing artwork _____

WHAT'S WORSE:
THE KNOWN OR THE UNKNOWN?

KNOWN PERILS	RATING
Death	_____
Taxes	_____
Monsanto	_____
Holidays	_____
Student loans	_____
Sexism	_____
Headaches	_____
Traffic	_____
Diarrhea	_____
Anti-vaxxers	_____
Job loss	_____
TOTAL	_____

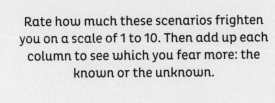

Rate how much these scenarios frighten you on a scale of 1 to 10. Then add up each column to see which you fear more: the known or the unknown.

UNKNOWN PERILS	RATING
Nuclear war	
Messy divorce	
Aliens	
Ghosts	
Car accidents	
Shark attacks	
Lightning strike	
False imprisonment	
House fire	
Food poisoning	
Burst appendix	
TOTAL	

··· ANXIOUS ···
SLEEP STYLES

Ah, slumber. The perfect escape from the waking misery of daily life. That is, unless your worries follow you into the Land of Nod to make for a fretful night's sleep. Review the anxious sleep styles below and check off all that apply to your nocturnal turmoil.

☐ **STARFISH**

The only thing you make room for is pets

☐ **THE SKIER**

You're barreling down a terrifying black diamond slope from hell in your nightmares

☐ **TINY ANGRY BALL**

How small can you get?

☐ **SPLAT**

Melted like the cheese on the nachos you stress-ate before bed

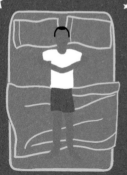

☐ **INSOMNIAC**

Your brain is running like a freight train full of snakes and explosives

☐ **TEAM EFFORT**

The revolving door of casual sex partners that make you feel even lonelier than sleeping by yourself

NIGHTMARE BINGO

Mark these bone-chilling themes as they appear in your bad dreams. Five in a row is a cry for help from your subconscious.

CHEATING	ANIMAL ATTACK	FIGHTING	FOOD ISSUES	BEING CHASED
SCREAM BUT NOTHING COMES OUT	CAN'T FIND SOMETHING	SOCIAL MEDIA FAIL	DEAD PETS	TRAVEL DISASTER
WORKPLACE	DROWNING		NAKED IN PUBLIC	INCEST
TEETH FALL OUT	TRYING TO RUN BUT CAN'T MOVE	REPEATS	SOMEONE TURNS INTO ANOTHER PERSON	END OF THE WORLD
PANIC ATTACK	BAD ROMANCE	NIGHTMARE WITHIN A NIGHTMARE	CONFRONT ABUSER	HIGH SCHOOL

NIGHTMARE
JOURNAL

RECURRING NIGHTMARE

_____

_____

_____

_____

_____

_____

WAKE UP IN A COLD SWEAT NIGHTMARE

_____

_____

_____

_____

_____

_____

ODDLY SEXY NIGHTMARE

_____
_____
_____
_____
_____
_____

SURPRISING NIGHTMARE

_____
_____
_____
_____
_____
_____

NIGHTMARE
JOURNAL

EMBARRASSING NIGHTMARE

_____

_____

_____

_____

_____

_____

MOST REALISTIC NIGHTMARE

_____

_____

_____

_____

_____

_____

_____

UNORIGINAL NIGHTMARE

_____

_____

_____

_____

_____

_____

INSPIRING NIGHTMARE

_____

_____

_____

_____

_____

_____

_____

HOPE FOR THE BEST BUT
ALWAYS EXPECT THE WORST

YOU MEET YOUR IDOL

Best-Case Scenario?

Worst-Case Scenario?

_____

_____

_____

_____

_____

_____

_____

_____

YOU INTERVIEW FOR YOUR DREAM JOB

Best-Case Scenario?

Worst-Case Scenario?

_____

_____

_____

_____

_____

_____

_____

_____

YOU GET A NEW PET

Best-Case Scenario?

Worst-Case Scenario?

_____

_____

_____

_____

_____

_____

_____

_____

YOU FORGET TO PACK SOCKS FOR YOUR VACATION

Best-Case Scenario?

Worst-Case Scenario?

_____

_____

_____

_____

_____

_____

_____

_____

··· WHICH ···
MONSTER ARE YOU?

Which monster are you? Which monsters
represent the people in your life?
Write a name next to each creature.

GLOBSTER

_____

Leave me alone—I'm tired.

AQUAPAL

_____

Please look at me
when I'm crying
to you.

ELECTROSLOTH

_____

I've watched
everything there is
to watch online.

BOTTLEBRO

_____

Years of
repressed rage
will explode all
at once.

SQUIRMY

_____

I keep my drama on a constant loop.

Some say the key to a good _____ is to take

1: THING

a deep _____ and focus on things

2: ACTION

that make you feel _____ .

3: EMOTION

Let the _____ sun wake you. Listen to the sounds

4: ADJECTIVE

of _____ and _____ .

5: ANIMAL, PLURAL   6: INSECT, PLURAL

Say a(n) _____ affirmation.

7: ADJECTIVE

Tell yourself, "I will _____ ."

8: GOAL

Then you can order in _____ and go

9: CUISINE TYPE

back to bed.

MASH

M = Mental institution   A = Attic of shame   S = Ship lost at sea   H = Hilltop cult

SPOUSE

1. _____
2. _____
3. A literal doormat
4. Your first celebrity crush
5. Reality television star
6. Adult child of an alcoholic

NUMBER OF KIDS

1. _____
2. _____
3. Negative three
4. One too many
5. TLC show levels
6. See: FUTURE PET

TRANSPORTATION

1. _____
2. _____
3. Awkwardly silent Lyft rides
4. '97 Chevy Cavalier
5. Hamster wheel
6. Ill-fitting shoes

CAREER

1. _____
2. _____
3. Murder clown
4. Ugh, *that* guy
5. Multilevel marketing
6. Cat herder

FUTURE PET

1. _____
2. _____
3. Geriatric cat
4. Skunk with removed stink gland
5. Yourself in *The Sims*
6. Sugar glider

SALARY

1. _____
2. _____
3. Processed sugar
4. Bitcoin
5. Moonshine
6. Tears of your enemies

HOW TO PLAY MASH

Close your eyes and draw a spiral or series of tally marks in the space provided until someone you care about begs you to stop. Count your spirals or tallies and use that number to go through each category to see what lies ahead on your life path.

BINGO! BINGO! BINGO!

Mark the symptoms of depression you have experienced.
Five in a row means you need to call and vent to the
emotional dumping ground of your choosing.

QUITTING JOB	YELLING AT A STRANGER	INSOMNIA	EATING FROM A CAN	HATING YOURSELF IN YOUR FAVORITE OUTFIT
SAME SONG ON REPEAT FOR A WEEK	SADSTURBATION	BUG INFESTATION	SOCIAL MEDIA FIGHT	WATCHING 6 SEASONS IN 4 DAYS
CRYING IN YOUR SLEEP	CHRONIC PAIN		20 BROWSER TABS	CRYING IN FRONT OF YOUR BOSS
WHAT IS SEX?	FIRED	BLAMING EVERYONE	CEREAL WITH WATER	GOING OUT, BUT TALKING ABOUT DEPRESSION ALL NIGHT
AMAZON PRIME ACCOUNT	RAGE SCREAM	BLOWING YOUR SAVINGS	NEW PET	MULTIPLE MORNING ALARMS

SOLIDLY Middle Class WHISKEY

CONNECT YOUR DEPRESSION TO
KEVIN BACON
(IN 6 MOVES OR LESS)

··· KARAOKE ···
CRIES FOR HELP

Song	Artist
Crazy	Patsy Cline
Everybody Hurts	R.E.M.
Hurt	Nine Inch Nails
I Can't Make You Love Me	Bonnie Raitt
I Will Follow You into the Dark	Death Cab for Cutie
Last Resort	Papa Roach
My Heart Will Go On	Celine Dion
Tears in Heaven	Eric Clapton

ADD YOUR OWN

SONG	ARTIST

CHARADE PROMPTS

THAT WILL UPSET PEOPLE AT THE PARTY

- Bill Cosby
- Feline AIDS
- *The Sopranos* finale
- Westboro Baptist Church
- #MeToo
- Midlife crisis

- Credit card debt
- *E. coli*
- Artificial intelligence
- Amy Winehouse
- Ponzi scheme
- Lice

ADD YOUR OWN

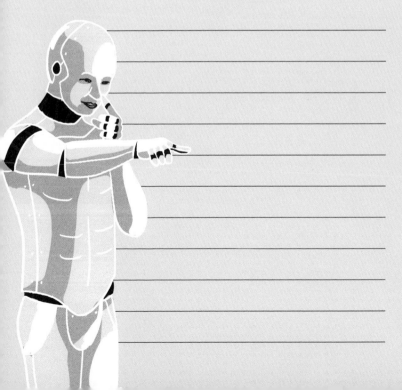

COLORING BREAK!

DRINKING ALONE VINEYARDS

Drinking Alone
VINEYARDS
——
SELF-
ISOLATION
Syrah

Drinking Alone
VINEYARDS
——
PLOTTING
EVIL
Chardonnay

Drinking Alone
VINEYARDS
——
PRIVATE
HELL
Sauvignon Blanc

A dynamic offering of deeply dysfunctional,
sumptuous wines dedicated to solitary drinkers.

MATCH EACH WORD

••• WITH THE DEFINITION •••

Word	Definition
EMPOWERMENT	Vehicle for transporting terrible smells and sounds to your senses
SUNGLASSES	Something that happens multiple times during sleeping hours in between nightmares
RESPONSIBILITY	A state of visual perfection and universal desirability that which you will never achieve
INSURANCE	A place to sit and contemplate the utter uselessness of your education
AIR	The feeling of ultimate control that accompanies the violent murder of household insects
BEAUTY	Being footloose and fancy-free with online purchases and sexual partners
AWAKEN	Health extortion
DESK	The hypothetical reason for being, doing, and saying the things that make you happy
IMPULSIVE	An unavoidable burden that should not be taken on voluntarily
PASSION	Advantageous tool for concealing puffy eyes after crying in public

FIND THE WORDS

••• THAT DON'T BELONG •••

fairness

equality

decency

patriarchy

soothe

relax

news

tranquil

thrill

employment

adventure

pleasure

family

easy

effortless

painless

healthy

natural

pure

technology

freedom

joy

debt

prosperity

binge

control

moderation

pride

contentment

security

affirmation

Instagram

good

harmless

people

rational

honesty

trust

virtue

politics

TRUE CRIME
• • • DOCUMENTARIES • • •

Rank these shows from 1 to 10 based on how much they reaffirm your lack of faith in humanity.

_____ *The Staircase*

_____ *Making a Murderer*

_____ *The Keepers*

_____ *Wild Wild Country*

_____ *The Jinx*

_____ *Paradise Lost* trilogy

_____ *O. J.: Made in America*

_____ *Dear Zachary*

_____ *There's Something Wrong with Aunt Diane*

_____ *Cropsey*

SAD-ISFYING

• • • STORIES • • •

Rank these classic tales of heartwarming tragedy from your childhood based on how much they scratch your itch for a good cry.

_____ *The Velveteen Rabbit*

_____ *"The Little Match Girl"*

_____ *"The Ugly Duckling"*

_____ *Charlotte's Web*

_____ *Old Yeller*

_____ *Where the Red Fern Grows*

_____ *Where the Wild Things Are*

_____ *Love You Forever*

_____ *The Giving Tree*

_____ *The Little Prince*

_____ *The Land Before Time*

_____ *My Girl*

_____ *Bambi*

_____ *E.T.*

_____ *All Dogs Go to Heaven*

_____ *The Lion King*

_____ *The Neverending Story*

_____ *Watership Down*

BOREDOM JAR

Use these suggestions or write your own and put them in a jar. Slather some glue all over the jar and decorate it with glitter or cigarette ashes or whatever strikes your fancy. Pull one suggestion out to use when feeling listless.

Look at your email inbox until an email arrives.

Plant a tree and then promptly cut it down because fuck that tree.

Go to the library to slip porno mags in between the serious books.

Go to a Little League game and yell at the players.

Write down all the people pissing you off and why.

Bake a cake and eat it with your hands.

Abandon your home and live off the grid.

Send a fake ransom note to your loved ones for your safe return.

Dress in all white and recruit members for a cult that doesn't exist.

Visualize helping people less fortunate than you, but then don't.

Write your own obituary so no one fucks it up.

Plan a trip you can't afford.

• • • PLAN A • • •
FIELD TRIP

Go outside but also make sure to bring your phone so you can continue to stare at your screen the entire time. Here are some examples of places you can go to stare at your phone while you get some fresh air.

THE BEACH

THE PARK

THE GRAND CANYON

A PICNIC

A ROOFTOP PARTY

THE DEEPEST, DARKEST FOREST

A URINE-DRENCHED WATER PARK

MOUNT EVEREST

A MUSIC FESTIVAL

YOUR OWN BACKYARD

A URINE-DRENCHED MUNICIPAL POOL

THE DESERT

THE HEART OF THE JUNGLE

A PLACE WITH A LOT OF BEES

A PLACE WITH A MODERATE AMOUNT OF BEES

THE OPEN SEA

HOPE FOR THE BEST BUT
ALWAYS EXPECT
THE WORST

A LONG-LOST RELATIVE DIES AND LEAVES YOU THEIR ENTIRE FORTUNE

Best-Case Scenario?   Worst-Case Scenario?

_____   _____

_____   _____

_____   _____

_____   _____

YOU FIND $20 IN AN OLD WINTER JACKET

Best-Case Scenario?

Worst-Case Scenario?

_____

_____

_____

_____

_____

_____

_____

_____

YOU MEET AN ATTRACTIVE PERSON FROM A DATING APP FOR DRINKS

Best-Case Scenario?

Worst-Case Scenario?

_____

_____

_____

_____

_____

_____

_____

_____

YOUR SHITTY ROOMMATE FINALLY MOVES OUT

Best-Case Scenario?

Worst-Case Scenario?

_____

_____

_____

_____

_____

_____

_____

_____

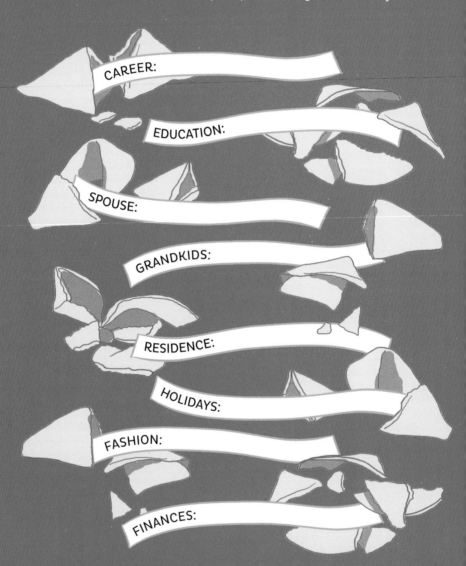

PARENTS'
CRUSHED DREAMS

Fill in the expectations your parental figures had for you.

CAREER:

EDUCATION:

SPOUSE:

GRANDKIDS:

RESIDENCE:

HOLIDAYS:

FASHION:

FINANCES:

RAGE SOUP

Stew in your juices to make a tasty broth of bottled-up rage.

AGITATE   HATRED   SILENCE
ANGER   HOSTILE   TANTRUM
ANIMOSITY   MADNESS   TEMPER
BITTER   OUTBURST   UPSET
FIRE   RESENT   WRATH
FURY   SCORN   YELL

COLORING BREAK!

TOPIARY GARDEN

• • • OF TENSION • • •

Show us your panic level by coloring the topiaries.

PARENTAL FIGURES

HEALTH WORRIES

DARK GREEN: This makes me sad.
LIGHT GREEN: This makes me worry.
YELLOW: This makes me furious.

BROWN: This makes me sick.
BLACK: This makes me dissociate from reality.

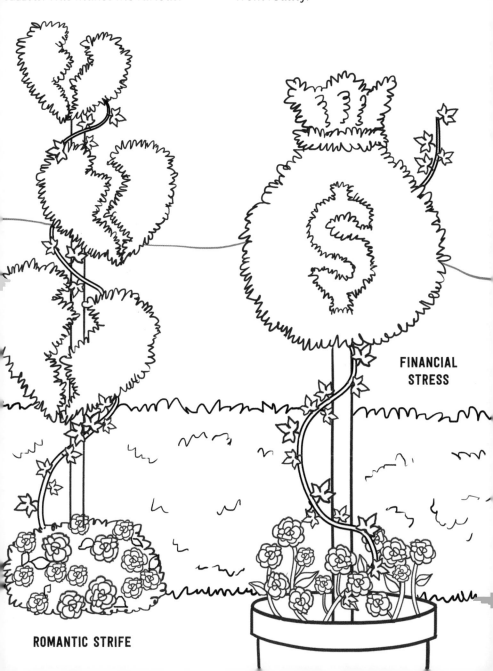

FINANCIAL STRESS

ROMANTIC STRIFE

··· ONE-WEEK ···
SELF-CARE CHALLENGE

MONDAY
Watch a movie & review it:

_____
_____
_____

TUESDAY
Watch the sequel & review it:

_____
_____
_____

WEDNESDAY
Watch the trilogy & review it:

_____
_____
_____

THURSDAY
Watch the prequel & review it:

_____
_____
_____

FRIDAY

Watch the remake & review it:

_____

_____

_____

SATURDAY

Watch the movie in 3-D & review it:

_____

_____

_____

SUNDAY

Watch your pet watch the movie & review it:

_____

_____

_____

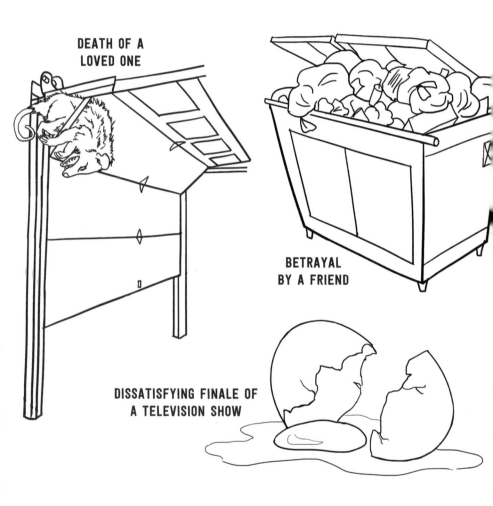

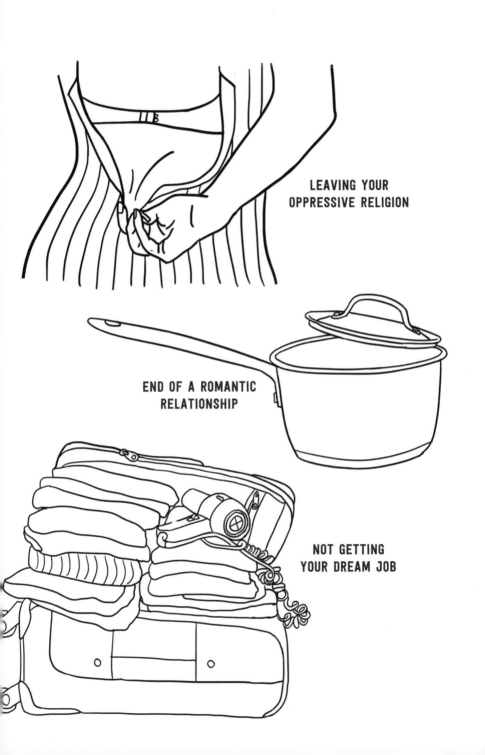

LEAVING YOUR
OPPRESSIVE RELIGION

END OF A ROMANTIC
RELATIONSHIP

NOT GETTING
YOUR DREAM JOB

HOPE FOR THE BEST BUT
• • • ALWAYS EXPECT THE WORST • • •

YOU SHIT YOURSELF IN PUBLIC

Best-Case Scenario?

Worst-Case Scenario?

_____

_____

_____

_____

_____

_____

_____

_____

YOU MOVE BACK IN WITH YOUR PARENTS

Best-Case Scenario?

Worst-Case Scenario?

_____

_____

_____

_____

_____

_____

_____

_____

YOUR POWER IS SHUT OFF

Best-Case Scenario?

Worst-Case Scenario?

_____

_____

_____

_____

_____

_____

_____

_____

YOUR BIRTHDAY CAKE BURNS DOWN YOUR HOUSE

Best-Case Scenario?

Worst-Case Scenario?

_____

_____

_____

_____

_____

_____

_____

_____

PEACEFUL THOUGHTS

You will never have to pay another Blockbuster late fee.

•

Nothing really matters in the grand scheme of things.

•

They never did catch D. B. Cooper.

•

Liquor is legal in all 50 states.

•

One time you ripped the loudest, smelliest fart and no one was around to know.

•

You can always fake your own death.

•

Cheese exists.

•

You can't get chicken pox twice.

ADD YOUR OWN

GET STARTED ON YOUR
VISION BOARD

Think about your goals: Want to get a promotion? Get famous? Cure diseases? Envision these goals, but then be realistic and settle. Now you can grab an old magazine and start cutting out encouraging words like you're making a positive ransom note to your dreams. Glue everything to a poster board and roll your face in glitter. You're magic.

ITEMS NEEDED

Poster board

Scissors

Glue stick

Some old magazines

Our handy vision board materials for inspiration to get started!

QUESTIONS TO ASK YOURSELF

What are some goals you have that are easy and attainable?

What images and words represent your life?

Who do you want to put in their place?

REASONABLE DEBT

UGH

imposter syndrome

meh

BORED WITHOUT CHAOS

i miss u

FUNCTIONAL

mediocre

READING FACES

Having trouble picking up what people are putting down? Match their face and decode!

You just said something mean or messed-up.

They want you to finish this long story.

They were talking about you when you walked in.

They know you're lying about how you spent your day.

They were hoping you wouldn't talk to them but here you are!

They are about to dump you.

They found out about your sexual kinks.

You need to stop talking about yourself or they're going to explode on you.

You need to leave the room.

BY THE MINUTE

What horrifyingly inappropriate personal tidbits
can you divulge in a relatively short period of time?

15-MINUTE CONVERSATION

_____
_____
_____

30-MINUTE CONVERSATION

_____
_____
_____

45-MINUTE CONVERSATION

_____
_____
_____

60-MINUTE CONVERSATION

_____
_____
_____

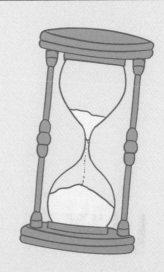

INTRODUCTION CARDS

Introduction cards are great for the things you're tired of explaining. Just pass them out when you meet people so they have fair warning!

LET'S PARTY!

I'm only fun when I'm on my third drink. After that . . .

YOU CAN PROBABLY TRUST ME

I can overcommit myself until I burn out and disappear.

WE SHOULD HANG OUT SOMETIME!

Maybe one day I'll be free. Not this year though.

WHO'S ALL GOING?

Other than you . . . who can I expect before I commit?

I'M BROKE

So don't invite me to anything that requires money.

I'M SORRY

In advance for whatever inadvertently hostile thing I may say or do in the future.

COLORING BREAK!

HEAR NO EVIL

Color in all the side effects from your medication that other people don't want to hear about!

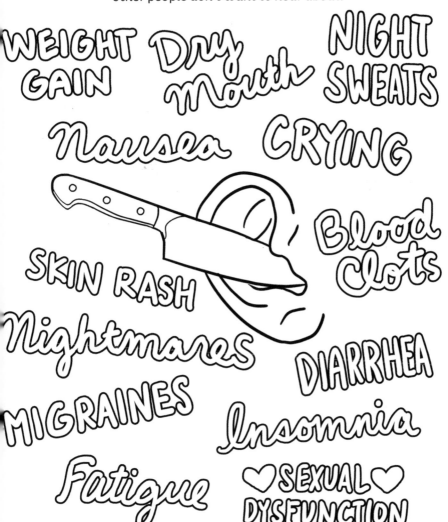

WEIGHT GAIN

Dry Mouth

NIGHT SWEATS

Nausea

CRYING

Blood Clots

SKIN RASH

Nightmares

DIARRHEA

MIGRAINES

Insomnia

Fatigue

♡SEXUAL♡ DYSFUNCTION

DIFFERENT WAYS

TO TELL PEOPLE YOU'RE FINE

I'm aces!

Things are excellent.

Living the dream, baby!

Just dandy!

I'm exceptional.

Five stars.

I'm doing great.

Not too shabby!

Outstanding!

I am top-notch.

Hunky-dory!

I'm the cat's pajamas.

Super-fucking-duper!

ADD YOUR OWN

PLACES TO CRY

THAT DON'T MAKE OTHER PEOPLE UNCOMFORTABLE

Weddings

Funerals

Shower

Rainstorm

Maternity ward

Bathroom

The ocean

Graduations

Haunted houses

The movies

Waterslides

ADD YOUR OWN

_____   _____

_____   _____

_____   _____

_____   _____

EXPLAIN TO SOMEONE YOU LIKE WHY
YOU CAN'T COME
TO THEIR BIRTHDAY PARTY

MENTAL HEALTH DAY
PUNCH CARD

CANCELLED PLANS

10 Cancelled Plans =
1 Night of Guilt-Free Solitude

FREQUENT SITTER

Give Yourself 1 Stamp for Each Period of **8 HOURS**
Spent Immobile to Earn **5 EXTRA POINTS** on Your BMI

MENTAL HEALTH DAYS

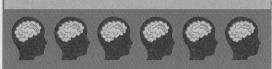

6 Days Calling Out of Work =
1 Complimentary Termination

COLORING BREAK!

MANTRA MADNESS

Forced positivity isn't the only path to tranquility.
Saying "no" can be a form of self-care too.

NAHHH

NEVER

Have you LOST Your fuckin' MIND?

Stop ASKING IF I'VE TRIED Yoga

YEAH, NO.

• • • GO BERSERK • • •
ON SOME BALLOONS

Write your problems on balloons and stab them all away! (Or go outside and release them to the mercy of a passing jet engine.)

JOB

BAD ADVICE

FEAR

COMPARE YOURSELF

In the digital age, it is now easier than ever to compare your life to those of your friends, acquaintances, and even strangers! Whether this makes you feel better or worse about your situation depends on the person you are stalking.

ROMANTIC RELATIONSHIPS

Person you envy: _____

Person you don't: _____

PROFESSIONAL ACCOMPLISHMENTS

Person you envy: _____

Person you don't: _____

SOCIAL LIFE

Person you envy: _____

Person you don't: _____

LIVING SITUATION

Person you envy: _____

Person you don't: _____

FAMILY BONDS

Person you envy: my kardachian

Person you don't: _____

PHYSICAL APPEARANCE

Person you envy: _____

Person you don't: _____

FINANCIAL STATUS

Person you envy: _____

Person you don't: _____

TRAVEL HISTORY

Person you envy: _____

Person you don't: _____

EMBARRASSING MOMENTS TO RECALL

 WHEN YOU'RE FEELING
A LITTLE TOO GOOD
ABOUT YOURSELF

WORK-RELATED

(e.g., that time you accidentally called your boss "Dad")

Shameful Moment: _____

_____

_____

PUBLIC SPACES

(e.g., that time you got into a shouting match with a manspreader on the train)

Shameful Moment: _____

_____

_____

LOVE LIFE

(e.g., that time you had uncontrollable diarrhea on a date at the bowling alley)

Shameful Moment: _____

_____

_____

FAMILY RELATIONS

(e.g., that time you had an epic meltdown in the JCPenney portrait studio)

Shameful Moment: _____

_____

_____

SOCIAL LIFE

(e.g., that time you passed out drunk at the party and urinated
all over the pile of coats on the bed)

Shameful Moment: _____

_____

_____

MISCELLANEOUS

(e.g., that time you accidentally spelled the recipient's
name incorrectly in an important email inquiry)

Shameful Moment: _____

_____

_____

WHAT YOU SHOULE

EXAMPLES:

Who hurt you?

•

Please never procreate.

•

Karma doesn't exist, but small
claims court sure does!

•

It's a shame you were only
skilled enough to fuck your way
to middle management.

•

May all your flights have
screaming infants on board!

•

You won't do well in prison.

•

You're the human equivalent
of Black Friday.

TO YOUR
**MICROMANAGING
BOSS**

TO YOUR
**PASSIVE-AGGRESSIVE
NEIGHBOR**

HAVE SAID INSTEAD

TO THE
SPINELESS COWARD
WHO GHOSTED

TO YOUR
OVERBEARING MOTHER

TO THAT
CREEPY CATCALLER

TO THE
**INCONSIDERATE
ASSHOLE**
ON YOUR COMMUTE

STAGES OF

GETTING DUMPED

Dumped again? Track your healing progress!

THIS HAS
TO BE A
MISTAKE

CRYING AND
CRYING AND
CRYING

I DON'T
WANT TO
LEAVE BED

WHO IS
THAT?

I PROMISE
WE CAN DO A
THREE-WAY

HONESTLY,
THEY
CAN KICK
ROCKS

UGH, I HAVE
TO LEAVE TO
GET STUFF

I DON'T
UNDERSTAND
HOW THIS IS
HAPPENING

REBOUND
SEX WHILE
CRYING

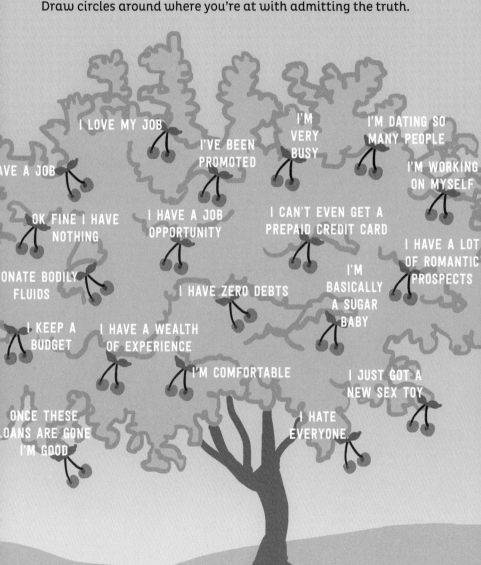

· · · QUILT OF · · ·
BAD MEMORIES

Find scraps of fabric to sew together for a truly horrifying blanket of misery with perhaps a few silver linings.

T-shirt from your ex's shitty band that at least opened for some actually decent bands

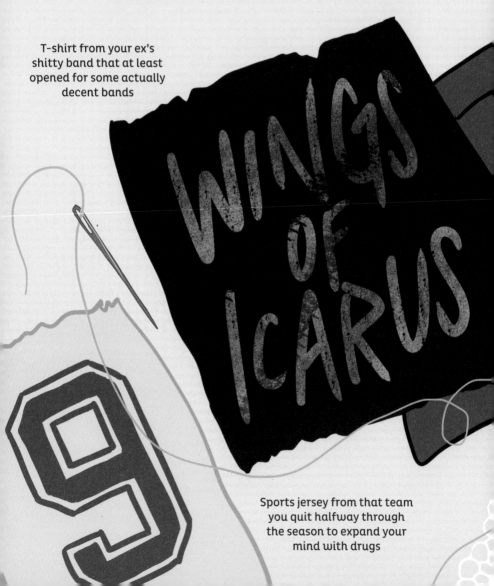

WINGS OF ICARUS

Sports jersey from that team you quit halfway through the season to expand your mind with drugs

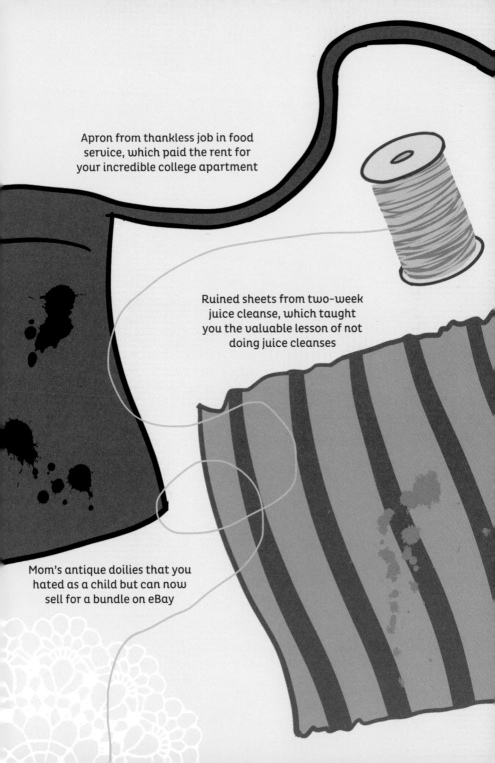

Apron from thankless job in food service, which paid the rent for your incredible college apartment

Ruined sheets from two-week juice cleanse, which taught you the valuable lesson of not doing juice cleanses

Mom's antique doilies that you hated as a child but can now sell for a bundle on eBay

COLORING BREAK!

SOME OF THE BRIDGES YOU HAVE BURNED

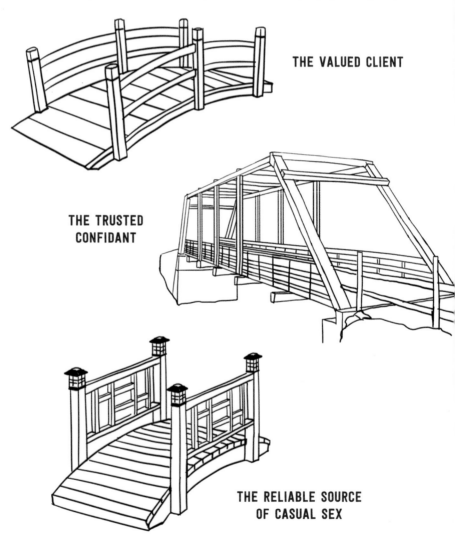

THE VALUED CLIENT

THE TRUSTED CONFIDANT

THE RELIABLE SOURCE OF CASUAL SEX

THE LOCAL PURVEYOR
OF ALCOHOL

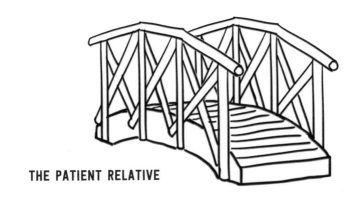

THE PATIENT RELATIVE

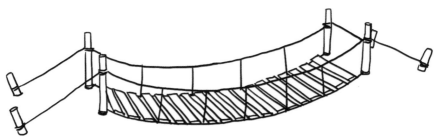

THE FRIENDLY COLLEAGUE

··· REASONS ···
YOU DRIFTED APART

REASON	PERSON WHO DRIFTED
You were never friends to begin with	
One of you ghosted	
Both of you ghosted	
They quit social media	
You ignored every event invite	
The Incident	
You were too sad for them to be around	
Friendzoning occurred	
You were too proud to apologize	
They were "too busy with work"	
One of you moved	
Jealous significant other	

DEPRESSING
• • • PASSWORD PROMPTS • • •

In case you forget your ID or password we will
ask for your secret answer to validate your identity.

What is the name of your favorite
unhealthy obsession?

Where did you meet your abusive ex?

Where did you spend your first
panic attack?

Best childhood bully?

Favorite historical villain?

What is the name of your
father's mistress?

What is the name of the last
street you threw up on?

The high school where you were
humiliated daily?

Your favorite dead pet?

Where you spent childhood
periods of isolation?

Your favorite food to binge?

Favorite sports domestic abuser?

At what age did you learn that
Santa isn't real?

Favorite movie to cry to?

PASSWORD:

TRUE or FALSE

You are easily your therapist's favorite patient.
TRUE | FALSE

All the people you knew in high school
are far more successful than you.
TRUE | FALSE

You can force someone to care about
you who currently does not.
TRUE | FALSE

Every negative thought you've ever had
TRUE | FALSE

A whirlwind romantic relationship will
cure all of your problems.
TRUE | FALSE

Food is a fine substitute for emotional support.
TRUE | FALSE

Your dream job really should have
fallen into your lap by now.
TRUE | FALSE

Past trauma is a valid excuse for shitty behavior.
TRUE | FALSE

They'll get theirs someday and you'll
be there to watch.
TRUE | FALSE

Everyone else remembers your most
awkward moments too.
TRUE | FALSE

NOURISHED RESENTMENTS

What do you feed your resentments to keep them alive and well?

EXAMPLES:

- revenge fantasies
- ruminating thoughts
- checking social media

ADD YOUR OWN:

_____

_____

_____

_____

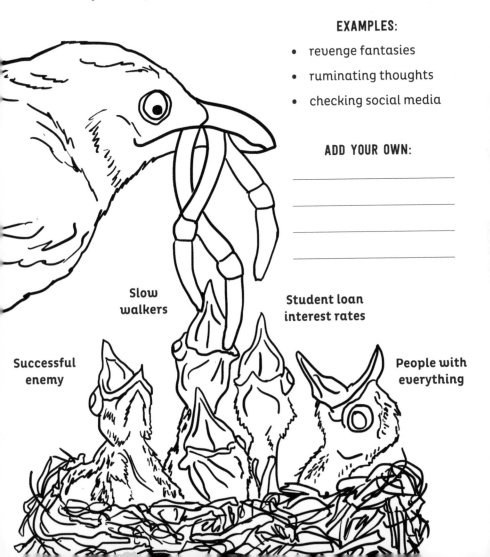

Slow walkers

Student loan interest rates

Successful enemy

People with everything

ALWAYS EXPECT
THE WORST

YOUR FACE BECOMES A VIRAL MEME

Best-Case Scenario?   Worst-Case Scenario?

_____   _____

_____   _____

_____   _____

_____   _____

YOU WIN TICKETS TO A CRUISE

Best-Case Scenario?

Worst-Case Scenario?

_____

_____

_____

_____

_____

_____

_____

_____

YOU WAKE UP AT 3 A.M. AND CAN'T GO BACK TO SLEEP

Best-Case Scenario?

Worst-Case Scenario?

_____

_____

_____

_____

_____

_____

_____

_____

YOUR BOSS WANTS YOU TO WRITE A SELF-ASSESSMENT

Best-Case Scenario?

Worst-Case Scenario?

_____

_____

_____

_____

_____

_____

_____

_____

DWELLING

$\cdots$ REPORT CARD $\cdots$

Time to be honest about your surroundings!

SUBJECT	GRADE
SMELL	A
TEMPERATURE	C
BRIGHTNESS OF LIGHTS	A
ENTERTAINMENT OPTIONS	A+
OVERALL AMBIANCE	B
PORNOGRAPHIC MATERIALS	no comment
ACCESS TO DRUG OF CHOICE	
SHEETS CLEANLINESS	

EXPLANATION OF MARKS

A - Excellent   B - Good   C - Satisfactory

D - Poor   F - Failure

SELF

• • • REPORT CARD • • •

This one might hurt a little.

SUBJECT	GRADE
EMOTIONAL STABILITY	C
SELF-ADVOCATION	A-
INTROSPECTION	A
SELECTIVE MEMORY	A+++
GRASP ON REALITY	C
GROOMING	B
INSTINCT TRUSTWORTHINESS	B
PHYSICAL FIGHT READINESS	A++++

EXPLANATION OF MARKS

A - Excellent B - Good C - Satisfactory

D - Poor F - Failure

REGRETS

REGRETS

REGRETS

REGRETS

YOU MADE IT!

You're not better because of this and
neither are we. But we all made it to the end
so that's something. This isn't supposed to be easy—
if it were, everyone would be happy all the time.
If you feel like your problems are more than you can
handle, here's a list of resources that could help you:

CRISIS TEXT LINE
Text CONNECT to 741741
in the United States.
crisistextline.org/textline

**NATIONAL SUICIDE
PREVENTION LIFELINE**
1-800-273-8255
Use that same number and press
"1" to reach the Veterans Crisis Line.

LIFENET
1-800-LIFENET

**AMERICAN FOUNDATION
FOR SUICIDE PREVENTION**
afsp.org

THE ICARUS PROJECT
theicarusproject.net

**NATIONAL ALLIANCE
ON MENTAL ILLNESS**
nami.org

ALCOHOLICS ANONYMOUS
212-647-1680

NARCOTICS ANONYMOUS
631-884-9500 and
212-929-6262

TREVOR LIFELINE
1-866-488-7386